THE
AMO

SELECTED BIRD
POEMS OF
ELIZABETH BARRETT BROWNING

With Illustrations by

ARCHIBALD THORBURN

Read & Co.

Copyright © 2021 Ragged Hand

This edition is published by Ragged Hand,
an imprint of Read & Co.

This book is copyright and may not be
reproduced or copied in any way without the
express permission of the publisher in writing.

British Library Cataloguing-in-Publication Data
A catalogue record for this book is available
from the British Library.

Read & Co. is part of Read Books Ltd.
For more information visit
www.readandcobooks.co.uk

CONTENTS

ILLUSTRATIONS

———————

ELIZABETH BARRETT BROWNING

———

By John William Cousin

A Poetess, was the daughter of Edward Barrett Moulton Barrett, who assumed the last name on succeeding to the estates of his grandfather in Jamaica. She was born at Coxhoe Hall, Durham, but spent her youth at Hope End, near Great Malvern. While still a child she showed her gift, and her first published work was 50 copies of a juvenile epic, on the Battle of Marathon. She was educated at home, but owed her profound knowledge of Greek and much mental stimulus to her early friendship with the blind scholar, Hugh Stuart Boyd, who was a neighbour. At the age of 15 she met with an injury to her spine which confined her to a recumbent position for several years, and from the effects of which she never fully recovered.

In 1826 she published anonymously *An Essay on Mind and Other Poems*. Shortly afterwards the abolition of slavery, of which he had been a disinterested supporter, considerably reduced Mr. Barrett's means: he accordingly disposed of his estate and removed with his family first to Sidmouth and afterwards to London. At the former Miss Barrett wrote *Prometheus Bound* (1833). After her removal to London she fell into delicate health, her lungs being threatened. This did not, however, interfere with her literary labours, and she contributed to various periodicals *The Romaunt of Margaret*, *The Romaunt of the Page*, *The Poet's Vow*, and other pieces. In 1838 appeared *The Seraphim and Other Poems* (including "Cowper's Grave.") Shortly thereafter the death, by drowning, of her favourite brother gave a serious shock to her already fragile health, and for a time she hovered between life and death. Eventually, however, she regained strength, and meanwhile her fame was growing. The publication about 1841 of *The Cry of the Children* gave it a great impulse, and about the same time she contributed some critical papers in prose to R. H. Horne's *New Spirit of the Age*. In 1844 she published two vols. of *Poems (UK)*, *A Drama of Exile, and other Poems* (US) which comprised "The Drama of Exile," "Vision of Poets," and "Lady Geraldine's Courtship." In 1845 she met for the first time her future husband, Robert Browning. Their courtship and marriage, owing to her delicate health and the extraordinary objections entertained by Mr. Barrett to the marriage of any of his children, were carried out under somewhat peculiar and romantic circumstances. After a private marriage and a secret departure from her home, she accompanied her husband to Italy, which became her home almost continuously until her death, and with the political aspirations of which she and her husband both thoroughly identified themselves. The union proved one of unalloyed happiness to both, though it was never forgiven by Mr. Barrett. In her new circumstances her strength greatly increased. Her husband and she settled in Florence, and there she wrote *Casa Guidi Windows* (1851)—by many considered her strongest work—under the inspiration of the Tuscan struggle for liberty. *Aurora Leigh*, her largest, and perhaps the most popular of her longer poems, appeared in 1856. In 1850 *The Sonnets from the Portuguese*—the history of her own love-story, thinly disguised by its title—had appeared. In 1860 she issued a collected edition of her poems under the title, *Poems before Congress*. Soon thereafter her health underwent a change for the worse; she gradually lost strength, and died on June 29, 1861. She is generally considered the greatest of English poetesses. Her works are full of tender and delicate, but also of strong and deep, thought. Her own sufferings, combined with her moral and intellectual strength, made her the champion of the suffering and oppressed wherever she found them. Her gift was essentially lyrical, though much of her work was not so in form. Her weak points are the lack of compression, an occasional somewhat obtrusive mannerism, and frequent failure both in metre and rhyme. Though not nearly the equal of her husband in force of intellect and the higher qualities of the poet, her works had, as might be expected on a comparison of their respective subjects and styles, a much earlier and wider acceptance with the general public. Mrs. Browning was a woman of singular nobility and charm, and though not beautiful, was remarkably attractive. Miss Mitford thus describes her as a young woman: "A slight, delicate figure, with a shower of dark curls falling on each side of a most expressive face; large, tender eyes, richly fringed by dark eyelashes, and a smile like a sunbeam."

Elizabeth Barrett Browning

BIRDS
AND POETS

An Excerpt by John Burroughs

It might almost be said that the birds are all birds of the poets and of no one else, because it is only the poetical temperament that fully responds to them. So true is this, that all the great ornithologists—original namers and biographers of the birds—have been poets in deed if not in word. Audubon is a notable case in point, who, if he had not the tongue or the pen of the poet, certainly had the eye and ear and heart—"the fluid and attaching character"—and the singleness of purpose, the enthusiasm, the unworldliness, the love, that characterize the true and divine race of bards.

So had Wilson, though perhaps not in as large

a measure; yet he took fire as only a poet can. While making a journey on foot to Philadelphia, shortly after landing in this country, he caught sight of the red-headed woodpecker flitting among the trees,—a bird that shows like a tricolored scarf among the foliage,—and it so kindled his enthusiasm that his life was devoted to the pursuit of the birds from that day. It was a lucky hit. Wilson had already set up as a poet in Scotland, and was still fermenting when the bird met his eye and suggested to his soul a new outlet for its enthusiasm.

The very idea of a bird is a symbol and a suggestion to the poet. A bird seems to be at the top of the scale, so vehement and intense is his life,—large-brained, large-lunged, hot, ecstatic, his frame charged with buoyancy and his heart with song. The beautiful vagabonds, endowed with every grace, masters of all climes, and knowing no bounds,—how many human aspirations are realized in their free, holiday lives, and how many suggestions to the poet in their flight and song!

Indeed, is not the bird the original type and

teacher of the poet, and do we not demand of the human lark or thrush that he "shake out his carols" in the same free and spontaneous manner as his winged prototype? Kingsley has shown how surely the old minnesingers and early ballad-writers have learned of the birds, taking their key-note from the blackbird, or the wood-lark, or the throstle, and giving utterance to a melody as simple and unstudied. . . . Or the best lyric pieces, how like they are to certain bird-songs!—clear, ringing, ecstatic, and suggesting that challenge and triumph which the outpouring of the male bird contains. (Is not the genuine singing, lyrical quality essentially masculine?) Keats and Shelley, perhaps more notably than any other English poets, have the bird organization and the piercing wild-bird cry. This, of course, is not saying that they are the greatest poets, but that they have preëminently the sharp semi-tones of the sparrows and the larks.

But when the general reader thinks of the birds of the poets, he very naturally calls to mind the renowned birds, the lark and the nightingale, Old World melodists, embalmed in Old World poetry, but occasionally appearing on these shores, transported in the verse of some callow singer. . .

AN EXCERPT FROM
Birds and Poets – And Other Papers, 1877

THE SWAN'S NEST
AMONG THE REEDS

SELECTED BIRD POEMS OF
ELIZABETH BARRETT BROWNING

Bluetits

AN ISLAND

———————

New Monthly Magazine, January, 1837

"All goeth but Goddis will." —OLD POET.

I

My dream is of an island-place
    Which distant seas keep lonely;
A little island on whose face
    The stars are watchers only:
Those bright still stars! they need not seem
Brighter or stiller in my dream.

II

An island full of hills and dells,
    All rumpled and uneven
With green recesses, sudden swells,
    And odorous valleys driven
So deep and straight, that always there
The wind is cradled to soft air.

III

Hills running up to heaven for light
    Through woods that half-way ran,
As if the wild earth mimicked right
    The wilder heart of man:
Only it shall be greener far
And gladder than hearts ever are.

IV

More like, perhaps, that mountain piece
     Of Dante's paradise,
Disrupt to an hundred hills like these,
     In falling from the skies;
Bringing within it, all the roots
Of heavenly trees and flowers and fruits.

V

For—saving where the grey rocks strike
     Their javelins up the azure,
Or where deep fissures, miser-like
     Hoard up some fountain treasure,
(And e'en in them, stoop down and hear,
Leaf sounds with water in your ear,)—

VI

The place is all awave with trees,
    Limes, myrtles purple-beaded,
Acacias having drunk the lees
    Of the night-dew, faint-headed,
And wan grey olive-woods which seem
The fittest foliage for a dream.

VII

Trees, trees on all sides! they combine
    Their plumy shades to throw,
Through whose clear fruit and blossom fine
    Whene'er the sun may go,
The ground beneath he deeply stains,
As passing through cathedral panes.

VIII

But little needs this earth of ours
        That shining from above her,
When many Pleiades of flowers
        (Not one lost) star her over,
The rays of their unnumbered hues
Being all refracted by the dews.

IX

Wide-petalled plants that boldly drink
        The Amreeta of the sky,
Shut bells that dull with rapture sink,
        And lolling buds, half shy;
I cannot count them, but between
Is room for grass and mosses green,

X

And brooks, that glass in different strengths
    All colours in disorder.
Or, gathering up their silver lengths
    Beside their winding border,
Sleep, haunted through the slumber hidden,
By lilies white as dreams in Eden.

XI

Nor think each arched tree with each
    Too closely interlaces
To admit of vistas out of reach,
    And broad moon-lighted places
Upon whose sward the antlered deer
May view their double image clear.

XII

For all this island's creature-full,
　　(Kept happy not by halves)
Mild cows, that at the vine-wreaths pull,
　　Then low back at their calves
With tender lowings, to approve
The warm mouths milking them for love.

XIII

Free gamesome horses, antelopes,
　　And harmless leaping leopards,
And buffaloes upon the slopes,
　　And sheep unruled by shepherds:
Hares, lizards, hedgehogs, badgers, mice,
Snakes, squirrels, frogs, and butterflies.

XIV

And birds that live there in a crowd,
    Horned owls, rapt nightingales,
Larks bold with heaven, and peacocks proud,
    Self-sphered in those grand tails;
All creatures glad and safe, I deem.
No guns nor springes in my dream!

XV

The island's edges are a-wing
    With trees that overbranch
The sea with song-birds welcoming
    The curlews to green change;
And doves from half-closed lids espy
The red and purple fish go by.

XVI

One dove is answering in trust
    The water every minute,
Thinking so soft a murmur must
    Have her mate's cooing in it:
So softly does earth's beauty round
Infuse itself in ocean's sound.

XVII

My sanguine soul bounds forwarder
    To meet the bounding waves;
Beside them straightway I repair,
    To live within the caves:
And near me two or three may dwell
Whom dreams fantastic please as well.

XVIII

Long winding caverns, glittering far
        Into a crystal distance!
Through clefts of which, shall many a star
        Shine clear without resistance,
And carry down its rays the smell
Of flowers above invisible.

XIX

I said that two or three might choose
        Their dwelling near mine own:
Those who would change man's voice and use,
        For Nature's way and tone—
Man's veering heart and careless eyes,
For Nature's steadfast sympathies.

XX

Ourselves to meet her faithfulness,
    Shall play a faithful part;
Her beautiful shall ne'er address
    The monstrous at our heart:
Her musical shall ever touch
Something within us also such.

XXI

Yet shall she not our mistress live,
    As doth the moon of ocean,
Though gently as the moon she give
    Our thoughts a light and motion:
More like a harp of many lays,
Moving its master while he plays.

XXII

No sod in all that island doth
    Yawn open for the dead;
No wind hath borne a traitor's oath;
    No earth, a mourner's tread;
We cannot say by stream or shade,
'I suffered here—was

XXIII

Our only "farewell" we shall laugh
    To shifting cloud or hour,
And use our only epitaph
    To some bud turned a flower:
Our only tears shall serve to prove
Excess in pleasure or in love.

XXIV

Our fancies shall their plumage catch
        From fairest island-birds,
Whose eggs let young ones out at hatch,
        Born singing! then our words
Unconsciously shall take the dyes
Of those prodigious fantasies.

XXV

Yea, soon, no consonant unsmooth
        Our smile-tuned lips shall reach;
Sounds sweet as Hellas spake in youth
        Shall glide into our speech:
(What music, certes, can you find
As soft as voices which are kind?)

XXVI

And often, by the joy without
    And in us, overcome,
We, through our musing, shall let float
    Such poems,—sitting dumb,—
As Pindar might have writ if he
Had tended sheep in Arcady;

XXVII

Or Æschylus—the pleasant fields
    He died in, longer knowing;
Or Homer, had men's sins and shields
    Been lost in Meles flowing;
Or Poet Plato, had the undim
Unsetting Godlight broke on him.

XXVIII

Choose me the cave most worthy choice,
    To make a place for prayer,
And I will choose a praying voice
    To pour our spirits there:
How silverly the echoes run!
Thy will be done,—thy will be done.

XXIX

Gently yet strangely uttered words!
    They lift me from my dream;
The island fadeth with its swards
    That did no more than seem:
The streams are dry, no sun could find—
The fruits are fallen, without wind.

XXX

So oft the doing of God's will
    Our foolish wills undoeth!
And yet what idle dream breaks ill,
    Which morning-light subdueth?
And who would murmur and misdoubt,
When God's great sunrise finds him out?

Spotted Flycatchers

Wood-Pigeon, or Ring-Dove

MY DOVES

The Seraphim, and Other Poems, 1838

" O Weisheit! Du red'st
wie eine Taube!" —GOETHE.

MY little doves have left a nest
   Upon an Indian tree
Whose leaves fantastic take their rest
   Or motion from the sea;
For ever there the sea-winds go
With sunlit paces to and fro.

The tropic flowers looked up to it,
    The tropic stars looked down,
And there my little doves did sit
    With feathers softly brown,
And glittering eyes that showed their right
To general Nature's deep delight.

And God them taught, at every close
    Of murmuring waves beyond
And green leaves round, to interpose
    Their choral voices fond,
Interpreting that love must be
The meaning of the earth and sea.

Fit ministers! Of living loves
    Theirs hath the calmest fashion,
Their living voice the likest moves
    To lifeless intonation,
The lovely monotone of springs
And winds and such insensate things.

My little doves were ta'en away
   From that glad nest of theirs
Across an ocean rolling gray
   And tempest-clouded airs:
My little doves, who lately knew
The sky and wave by warmth and blue.

And now, within the city prison,
   In mist and chillness pent,
With sudden upward look they listen
   For sounds of past content,
For lapse of water, swell of breeze,
Or nut-fruit falling from the trees.

The stir without the glow of passion,
   The triumph of the mart,
The gold and silver as they clash on
   Man's cold metallic heart,
The roar of wheels, the cry for bread, —
These only sounds are heard instead.

Yet still, as on my human hand
    Their fearless heads they lean,
And almost seem to understand
    What human musings mean,
(Their eyes with such a plaintive shine
Are fastened upwardly to mine!) —

Soft falls their chant as on the nest
    Beneath the sunny zone;
For love that stirred it in their breast
    Has not aweary grown,
And 'neath the city's shade can keep
The well of music clear and deep.

And love, that keeps the music, fills
    With pastoral memories;
All echoings from out the hills,
    All droppings from the skies,
All flowings from the wave and wind,
Remembered in their chant, I find.

So teach ye me the wisest part,
   My little doves! to move
Along the city-ways with heart
   Assured by holy love,
And vocal with such songs as own
A fountain to the world unknown.

'T was hard to sing by Babel's stream —
   More hard, in Babel's street:
But if the soulless creatures deem
   Their music not unmeet
For sunless walls — let us begin,
Who wear immortal wings within!

To me, fair memories belong
   Of scenes that used to bless,
For no regret, but present song
   And lasting thankfulness,
And very soon to break away,
Like types, in purer things than they.

I will have hopes that cannot fade,
    For flowers the valley yields;
I will have humble thoughts instead
    Of silent, dewy fields:
My spirit and my God shall be
My seaward hill, my boundless sea.

Nepalese Black-Headed Nun

Great Black-Backed Gull

THE SEA-MEW

_____

The Seraphim and Other Poems, 1838

AFFECTIONATELY
INSCRIBED TO M. E. H.

I

How joyously the young sea-mew
Lay dreaming on the waters blue
Whereon our little bark had thrown
A little shade, the only one,
But shadows ever man pursue.

II

Familiar with the waves and free
As if their own white foam were he,
His heart upon the heart of ocean
Lay learning all its mystic motion,
And throbbing to the throbbing sea.

III

And such a brightness in his eye
As if the ocean and the sky
Within him had lit up and nurst
A soul God gave him not at first,
To comprehend their majesty.

IV

We were not cruel, yet did sunder
His white wing from the blue waves under,
And bound it, while his fearless eyes
Shone up to ours in calm surprise,
As deeming us some ocean wonder.

V

We bore our ocean bird unto
A grassy place where he might view
The flowers that curtsey to the bees,
The waving of the tall green trees,
The falling of the silver dew.

VI

But flowers of earth were pale to him
Who had seen the rainbow fishes swim;
And when earth's dew around him lay
He thought of ocean's winged spray,
And his eye waxed sad and dim.

VII

The green trees round him only made
A prison with their darksome shade;
And drooped his wing, and mourned he
For his own boundless glittering sea—
Albeit he knew not they could fade.

VIII

Then One her gladsome face did bring,
Her gentle voice's murmuring,
In ocean's stead his heart to move
And teach him what was human love:
He thought it a strange, mournful thing.

IX

He lay down in his grief to die,
(First looking to the sea-like sky
That hath no waves) because, alas!
Our human touch did on him pass,
And, with our touch, our agony.

A Male Wheatear

THE POET
AND THE BIRD

A Drama of Exile, and Other Poems, 1844

Said a people to a poet—"Go out from among
    us straightway!
While we are thinking earthly things, thou singest
    of divine.
There's a little fair brown nightingale, who, sitting
    in the gateways
Makes fitter music to our ears than any song
    of thine!"
The poet went out weeping—the nightingale
    ceased chanting;
"Now, wherefore, O thou nightingale, is all thy
    sweetness done?"
I cannot sing my earthly things, the heavenly
    poet wanting,

Whose highest harmony includes the lowest
    under sun."
The poet went out weeping,—and died abroad,
    bereft there—
The bird flew to his grave and died, amid a thousand
    wails:—
And, when I last came by the place, I swear the music
    left there
Was only of the poet's song, and not the nightingale's.

PATIENCE
TAUGHT BY NATURE

———————

A Drama of Exile, and Other Poems, 1844

'O DREARY life,' we cry, 'O dreary life!'
And still the generations of the birds
Sing through our sighing, and the flocks and herds
Serenely live while we are keeping strife
With Heaven's true purpose in us, as a knife
Against which we may struggle! Ocean girds
Unslackened the dry land, savannah-swards
Unweary sweep, hills watch unworn, and rife
Meek leaves drop year]y from the forest-trees
To show, above, the unwasted stars that pass
In their old glory: O thou God of old,
Grant me some smaller grace than comes to these!—
But so much patience as a blade of grass
Grows by, contented through the heat and cold.

*Bewick's Swan, Whooper Swan
& Mute Swan (Adult and Young)*

THE ROMANCE OF
THE SWAN'S NEST

———————

A Drama of Exile, and other Poems, 1844

So the dreams depart,
So the fading phantoms flee,
And the sharp reality
Now must act its part.
          —WESTWOOD'S *Beads from a Rosary*

I

Little Ellie sits alone
'Mid the beeches of a meadow,
By a stream-side on the grass,
And the trees are showering down
Doubles of their leaves in shadow
On her shining hair and face.

II

She has thrown her bonnet by,
And her feet she has been dipping
  In the shallow water's flow:
  Now she holds them nakedly
In her hands, all sleek and dripping,
  While she rocketh to and fro.

III

Little Ellie sits alone,
And the smile she softly uses
  Fills the silence like a speech,
  While she thinks what shall be done,
And the sweetest pleasure chooses
  For her future within reach.

IV

Little Ellie in her smile
Chooses—"I will have a lover
    Riding on a steed of steeds:
    He shall love me without guile,
And to *him* I will discover
    The swan's nest among the reeds.

V

"And the steed shall be red-roan,
And the lover shall be noble,
    With an eye that takes the breath:
    And the lute he plays upon
Shall strike ladies into trouble,
    As his sword strikes men to death.

VI

"And the steed it shall be shod
All in silver, housed in azure,
   And the mane shall swim the wind;
   And the hoofs along the sod
Shall flash onward and keep measure,
   Till the shepherds look behind.

VII

"But my lover will not prize
All the glory that he rides in,
   When he gazes in my face:
   He will say, "O Love, thine eyes
Build the shrine my soul abides in,
   And I kneel here for thy grace!"

VIII

"Then, ay, then he shall kneel low,
With the red-roan steed anear him
    Which shall seem to understand,
    Till I answer, "Rise and go!
For the world must love and fear him
    Whom I gift with heart and hand."

IX

"Then he will arise so pale,
I shall feel my own lips tremble
    With a *yes* I must not say,
    Nathless maiden-brave, "Farewell,"
I will utter, and dissemble—
    "Light to-morrow with to-day!"

X

"Then he'll ride among the hills
To the wide world past the river,
   There to put away all wrong;
   To make straight distorted wills,
And to empty the broad quiver
   Which the wicked bear along.

XI

"Three times shall a young foot-page
Swim the stream and climb the mountain
   And kneel down beside my feet—
   "Lo, my master sends this gage,
Lady, for thy pity's counting!
   What wilt thou exchange for it?"

XII

"And the first time I will send
A white rosebud for a guerdon,
   And the second time, a glove;
   But the third time—I may bend
From my pride, and answer—"Pardon
   If he comes to take my love."

XIII

"Then the young foot-page will run,
Then my lover will ride faster,
   Till he kneeleth at my knee:
   "I am a duke's eldest son,
Thousand serfs do call me master,
   But, O Love, I love but *thee!* "

XIV

"He will kiss me on the mouth
Then, and lead me as a lover
    Through the crowds that praise his deeds;
    And when soul-tied by one troth,
Unto *him* I will discover
    That swan's nest among the reeds."

XV

Little Ellie, with her smile
Not yet ended, rose up gaily,
    Tied the bonnet, donned the shoe,
    And went homeward, round a mile,
Just to see, as she did daily,
    What more eggs were with the two.

XVI

Pushing through the elm-tree copse,
Winding up the stream, light-hearted,
   Where the osier pathway leads,
   Past the boughs she stoops—and stops.
Lo, the wild swan had deserted,
   And a rat had gnawed the reeds!

XVII

Ellie went home sad and slow.
If she found the lover ever,
   With his red-roan steed of steeds,
   Sooth I know not; but I know
She could never show him—never,
   That swan's nest among the reeds!

Robin

A DRAMA OF EXILE:
BIRD SPIRIT

———————

A Drama of Exile, and Other Poems, 1844

AN EXCERPT

Bird Spirit.

> I am the nearest nightingale
>   That singeth in Eden after you;
>   And I am singing loud and true,
> And sweet,—I do not fail.
>   I sit upon a cypress bough,
>   Close to the gate, and I fling my song
>   Over the gate and through the mail
> Of the warden angels marshalled strong,—
>   Over the gate and after you.
> And the warden angels let it pass,

Because the poor brown bird, alas,
    Sings in the garden, sweet and true.
And I build my song of high pure notes,
    Note over note, height over height,
    Till I strike the arch of the Infinite,
And I bridge abysmal agonies
With strong, clear calms of harmonies,—
And something abides, and something floats,
In the song which I sing after you.
Fare ye well, farewell!
The creature-sounds, no longer audible,
    Expire at Eden's door.
    Each footstep of your treading
Treads out some cadence which ye heard before.
    Farewell! the birds of Eden,
    Ye shall hear nevermore.

Pair of Redstarts

Red-Rumped Swallow & Swallow

PARAPHRASE ON ANACREON: ODE TO THE SWALLOW

Last Poems, 1862

Thou indeed, little Swallow,
A sweet yearly comer.
Art building a hollow
New nest every summer.
And straight dost depart
Where no gazing can follow.
Past Memphis, down Nile!
Ay! but love all the while
Builds his nest in my heart,
Through the cold winter-weeks:
And as one Love takes flight.
Comes another, O Swallow,
In an egg warm and white,
And another is callow.

And the large gaping beaks
Chirp all day and all night:
And the Loves who are older
Help the young and the poor Loves,
And the young Loves grown bolder
Increase by the score Loves—
Why, what can be done?
If a noise comes from one.
Can I bear all this rout of a hundred and more Loves?

BIANCA AMONG THE NIGHTINGALES

———————

Last Poems, 1862

I

The cypress stood up like a church
    That night we felt our love would hold,
And saintly moonlight seemed to search
    And wash the whole world clean as gold;
The olives crystallized the vales'
    Broad slopes until the hills grew strong:
The fireflies and the nightingales
    Throbbed each to either, flame and song.
The nightingales, the nightingales.

II

Upon the angle of its shade
    The cypress stood, self-balanced high;
Half up, half down, as double-made,
    Along the ground, against the sky.
And we, too! from such soul-height went
    Such leaps of blood, so blindly driven,
We scarce knew if our nature meant
    Most passionate earth or intense heaven.
The nightingales, the nightingales.

III

We paled with love, we shook with love,
    We kissed so close we could not vow;
Till Giulio whispered, 'Sweet, above
    God's Ever guarantees this Now.'
And through his words the nightingales
    Drove straight and full their long clear call,
Like arrows through heroic mails,
    And love was awful in it all.
The nightingales, the nightingales.

IV

O cold white moonlight of the north,
    Refresh these pulses, quench this hell!
O coverture of death drawn forth
    Across this garden-chamber. . . well!
But what have nightingales to do
    In gloomy England, called the free.
(Yes, free to die in! . . .) when we two
    Are sundered, singing still to me?
And still they sing, the nightingales.

V

I think I hear him, how he cried
   'My own soul's life' between their notes.
Each man has but one soul supplied,
   And that's immortal. Though his throat's
On fire with passion now, to *her*
   He can't say what to me he said!
And yet he moves her, they aver.
   The nightingales sing through my head.
The nightingales, the nightingales.

VI

He says to *her* what moves her most.
  He would not name his soul within
Her hearing,—rather pays her cost
  With praises to her lips and chin.
Man has but one soul, 'tis ordained,
  And each soul but one love, I add;
Yet souls are damned and love's profaned.
  These nightingales will sing me mad!
The nightingales, the nightingales.

VII

I marvel how the birds can sing.
   There's little difference, in their view,
Betwixt our Tuscan trees that spring
   As vital flames into the blue,
And dull round blots of foliage meant
   Like saturated sponges here
To suck the fogs up. As content
   Is *he* too in this land, 'tis clear.
And still they sing, the nightingales.

VIII

My native Florence! dear, forgone!
  I see across the Alpine ridge
How the last feast-day of Saint John
  Shot rockets from Carraia bridge.
The luminous city, tall with fire,
  Trod deep down in that river of ours,
While many a boat with lamp and choir
  Skimmed birdlike over glittering towers.
I will not hear these nightingales.

IX

I seem to float, *we* seem to float
  Down Arno's stream in festive guise;
A boat strikes flame into our boat,
  And up that lady seems to rise
As then she rose. The shock had flashed
  A vision on us! What a head,
What leaping eyeballs!—beauty dashed
  To splendour by a sudden dread.
And still they sing, the nightingales.

X

Too bold to sin, too weak to die;
    Such women are so. As for me,
I would we had drowned there, he and I,
    That moment, loving perfectly.
He had not caught her with her loosed
    Gold ringlets. . . rarer in the south. . .
Nor heard the 'Grazie tanto' bruised
    To sweetness by her English mouth.
And still they sing, the nightingales.

XI

She had not reached him at my heart
  With her fine tongue, as snakes indeed
Kill flies; nor had I, for my part,
  Yearned after, in my desperate need,
And followed him as he did her
  To coasts left bitter by the tide,
Whose very nightingales, elsewhere
  Delighting, torture and deride!
For still they sing, the nightingales.

XII

A worthless woman! mere cold clay
    As all false things are! but so fair,
She takes the breath of men away
    Who gaze upon her unaware.
I would not play her larcenous tricks
    To have her looks! She lied and stole,
And spat into my love's pure pyx
    The rank saliva of her soul.
And still they sing, the nightingales.

XIII

I would not for her white and pink,
   Though such he likes—her grace of limb,
Though such he has praised—nor yet, I think,
   For life itself, though spent with him,
Commit such sacrilege, affront
   God's nature which is love, intrude
'Twixt two affianced souls, and hunt
   Like spiders, in the altar's wood.
I cannot bear these nightingales.

XIV

If she chose sin, some gentler guise
   She might have sinned in, so it seems:
She might have pricked out both my eyes,
   And I still seen him in my dreams!
—Or drugged me in my soup or wine,
   Nor left me angry afterward:
To die here with his hand in mine
   His breath upon me, were not hard.
(Our Lady hush these nightingales!)

XV

But set a springe for *him,* 'mio ben',
   My only good, my first last love!—
Though Christ knows well what sin is, when
   He sees some things done they must move
Himself to wonder. Let her pass.
   I think of her by night and day.
Must *I* too join her . . . out, alas! . . .
   With Giulio, in each word I say!
And evermore the nightingales!

XVI

Giulio, my Giulio!—sing they so,
    And you be silent? Do I speak,
And you not hear? An arm you throw
    Round some one, and I feel so weak?
—Oh, owl-like birds! They sing for spite,
    They sing for hate, they sing for doom!
They'll sing through death who sing through night,
    They'll sing and stun me in the tomb—
The nightingales, the nightingales!

Nightingale

Pied Flycatcher

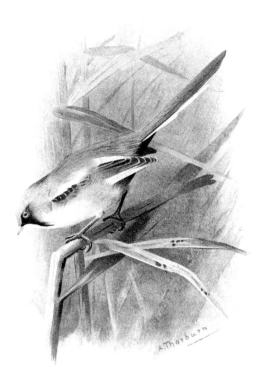

Bearded Titmouse

Printed in Great Britain
by Amazon